Kanto Region Field Guide

WELCOME TO KANTO!

If you're a thrill-seeking adventurer who loves Pokémon and competition, you're in the right place. Kanto is a paradise for Pokémon Trainers, breeders, Scientists, Coordinators, and of course, Pokémon! It is filled with ancient treasures, modern cities, and some of the most exciting Pokémon competitions, like the Indigo League Conference, the Grand Festival, the Battle Frontier, Pokémon Orienteering and Pokémon Races. To know the coolest places to go in Kanto, just turn the page!

GYMS & GYM LEADERS

Pokémon Trainers visiting Kanto will want to get in on all the battle action. A Gym battle is a good place to show your talent with your Pokémon pals. Gyms are located in major cities across the region. Each Gym has different rules, different battlefield designs, and a Gym Leader that focuses on a single Pokémon type. Challengers must journey from town to town to ask these very tough competitors for a chance to battle them to earn a special Gym badge. When a Trainer collects all eight badges in Kanto, he or she then qualifies to compete in the Pokémon League regional tournament—the Indigo League Championship! You'll find more on that competition in the pages of this book, but first, meet the eight great Gym Leaders of Kanto!

VISIT PEWTER GYM

BROCK: THE PEWTER GYM LEADER

LOCATION: Pewter City

OBSESSION: Rock-type Pokémon

Pewter Gym Leader Brock inherited the Gym from his troubled father, Flint. He's not just a Gym Leader though; he is also an awesome chef, budding Pokémon breeder, and caring older brother to his nine little brothers and sisters. Unlike his Gym, Brock's heart is not made of stone. He is a nurturer through and through. However, the one thing he can't seem to master is the fine art of wooing. He falls for every girl that walks by, but they all walk (and in some cases run) away from Brock, the wannabe Casanova.

BROCK'S POKÉMON:

Onix, Geodude, Zubat, Marshtomp, Forretress, Ludicolo, Croagunk, Chansey

PEWTER GYM

BADGE: Boulder Badge

BATTLE FOR THE BADGE: 2-on-2

Pewter Gym is solid—solid as a rock. It's a building made of boulders so big, they're often taller than the Trainers that visit it. The rocks fill a rust-color frame that comes to a point. The sign etched into the stone reads "Pewter Gym."

Two steps lead to the double doors where challengers enter. Inside, the walls are lined with stone brick. Brock, the Gym Leader, sits atop a rock altar waiting for challengers. The battlefield has rocky terrain, which gives Brock's Rock-type Pokémon pals an advantage.

PEWTER CITY

Just outside of Viridian Forest is Pewter City. Coming from the greenery in the woods, you can spot this city by its gray tone. It's gray because the area is made of stone.

In addition to the Pewter Gym, Trainers might also want to take their Pokémon for a rest at the local Pokémon Center. If you have an Electric-type Pokémon pal, you might also want to visit the old hydroelectric plant to give it a power boost.

VISIT CERULEAN GYM

MISTY, VIOLET, LILLY & DAISY: THE CERULEAN GYM LEADERS

LOCATION: Cerulean City

OBSESSION: Water-type Pokémon

The Cerulean Gym has not one, but four Gym Leaders. They are all sisters, but only three of them are stars. Lilly, Violet, and Daisy are also known as the Sensational Cerulean City Synchronized Swimming Sisters! Misty's sisters don't seem to think she can compete with them, but challengers at the Cerulean Gym should not make the same mistake and underestimate Misty. She is as fiery as her hair! And she is known to battle with a Mega-Evolved Gyarados—consider yourself warned.

MISTY'S POKÉMON:

Staryu, Starmie, Psyduck, Gyarados, Politoed, Togetic, Corsola, Azurill, Caserin, Horsea

CERULEAN GYM

BADGE: Cascade Badge

BATTLE FOR THE BADGE: 2-on-2

The Cerulean Gym's roof is round with pink and orange stripes. It looks almost like a delicious piece of candy! Swirled columns and a border of decorative waves line the stadium. A giant Dewgong plaque resides above a sign that reads "Cerulean Gym."

Inside, the arena is just as colorful, with yellow and white striped columns and pink walls with triangles. There is a giant pool with a tall diving board and stage door. During shows, large crowds watch in the stands, and spotlights follow Dewgong and the Synchronized Swimming Sisters' every move

Battles also take place in the same cool pool. Both the Gym Leader and challenger make their moves from floating docks in the water. Plus, the pool can be elevated during special events. Above the pool, windows let in lots of sunshine during the day. The basement boasts aquariums full of Water-type Pokémon.

CERULEAN CITY

This small city is a big draw for Trainers visiting Kanto. Cerulean City sits right on the ocean. A famous bright white lighthouse sits atop a cliff. There are lots of shops in the mall, including a machine shop. There is a beautiful park with a nice bench and perfectly mowed grass. There are buildings that reach a few floors above the tree line, but nothing too tall. Cerulean City might seem low key, but if you've come for the Cascade Badge, prepare for a lot of excitement!

VISIT VERMILION GYM

LT. SURGE: VERMILION GYM LEADER

LOCATION: Vermilion City

OBSESSION: Electric-type Pokémon

Lt. Surge is a huge muscle man who wears black boots and fingerless black gloves. His hair stands straight up in the air. He doesn't just leave the attacks to his Pokémon; he also bullies his opponents by calling them names like "baby." This Gym Leader can hurl insults that are even more shocking than the moves his Electric-type Pokémon pal Raichu performs on the battlefield. You have to have a thick skin and a smart battle strategy to challenge Lt. Surge.

LT. SURGE'S POKÉMON: Raichu

VERMILION GYM

BADGE: Thunder Badge

BATTLE FOR THE BADGE: 1-on-1

Lt. Surge's Gym is tall, just like him. It's a towering green building with big windows. It is decorated with big yellow lightning bolts that shoot up at the sky. The door is electric blue with a golden bolt on it.

When challengers enter the building, it's pitch-black, as if the electricity has been turned off. They're greeted by two shadowy figures who work for Lt. Surge.

Once the battle begins, the lights come on! The entire battlefield is lined with a row of bright stage lights. A burgundy border and white lines surround the rectangular arena. The judges have a special booth on the floor. Look up and you'll see more lightning bolts and an emblem of a red and orange ball with a bolt going through it.

VERMILION CITY

You know you've reached Vermilion City when you pass under the ornate green arch that proclaims the town's name. A path from the forest leads to the entrance in the wall that surrounds the city.

Vermilion City is quaint. Houses have picket fences and manicured lawns. Some buildings rise to multiple stories. The local Pokémon Center is quite large and very cute. It's a round, red building that looks like a face with two Poké Ball-looking eyes and a skylight nose. The door has a big orange "P" on it and bushy shrubs dot the entrance.

VISIT SAFFRON GYM

SABRINA: SAFFRON GYM LEADER

LOCATION: Saffron City

OBSESSION: Psychic-type Pokémon

Sabrina is one Gym Leader with two sides: the trouble-making Pokémon Trainer and the lonely little girl. Most people first meet the small child who wears a hat with a red bow and giggles constantly. But underneath that haunting laugh is a person tormented by her past and high on her own powers.

SABRINA'S POKÉMON:

Kadabra

Sabrina is sneaky and spooky. She glows with the incredible strength of the telekinetic powers she has practiced since she was young. Instead of playing, she worked hard to become the Psychic-type master that she is today. But nothing will ever fill the void of the friendships and bonds—even with her family— that she missed out on as a kid.

Because of this emptiness, she often transforms Trainers who loose matches at her Gym into dolls. She even turned her own mother into a toy. Then, she plays with the dolls in her mini model of Saffron City. It's a twisted time for challengers who aren't prepared to face this psychic whiz kid.

SAFFRON GYM

BADGE: Marsh Badge

BATTLE FOR THE BADGE: 1-on-1

The Saffron Gym is a strange, circular building whose roof comes down to the ground in many spiny legs. Inside the Gym are many golden, fluted columns with torches that give off a very warm light. But the reception at the Gym can be particularly cold. Behind an aqua-colored door, a room full of students wearing white lab coats work on their telekinetic powers. They are focused, trying to guess cards and bend spoons with their minds.

The battlefield where challengers face the formidable Sabrina is through purple double doors with Poké Balls painted on them. The room has purple pillars and two fiery cauldrons. Sabrina sits on a stage, in a red throne that looks like a flame. Behind the chair is a mural of a winged Poké Ball.

There is only one way to win the match with Sabrina: choose a Ghost-type Pokémon pal. It will have a type advantage over Sabrina's Pokémon friend Kadabra. For challengers unprepared to battle Sabrina, Saffron Gym might be the last thing they see as full-sized people.

SAFFRON CITY

Make your way to Saffron City by traveling through a dark and mysterious forest. That ought to prepare you for the strange sites at the Saffron Gym! The city itself is all lit up. Its streets are packed with shops, hotels, buildings and more! Saffron City has a lot in store for its visitors and citizens.

Follow the path lined with streetlights to the purple arch that reads, "Saffron City." However, you'll probably already know you've arrive by the impressive size of this metropolis.

ERIKA: CELADON GYM LEADER

LOCATION: Celadon City

OBSESSION: Grass-type Pokémon

People flock to Erika, enchanted by her unique scents. She's a one-of-a-kind Gym Leader who attracts many apprentices, and not just by aroma. Hard-working, smart, and caring, Erika manages her perfume shop, fragrance factory, and Gym with ease.

Although she carefully crafts so many perfumes, she loves nothing more than the sweet smell of victory! Erika accepts battle challenges from Trainers, as long as they too love fragrance. So, even if you have to hold your nose, your mouth has to praise perfume.

ERIKA'S POKÉMON:

Tangela, Weepinbell, Gloom

CELADON GYM

BADGE: Rainbow Badge

BATTLE FOR THE BADGE: 3-on-3

Fans of Vileplume might recognize the roof, with those big red petals and white polka dots. The Celadon Gym structure resembles the Flower Pokémon. A group of scouts in matching khaki uniforms and red scarves greets challengers at the door. For a Gym battle, you must register with one of the scouts at the front desk. Rejected challengers leave with more than a simple goodbye—their faces get stamped with a big red X.

Those who gain entry face Erika on a tree-lined battlefield. Friends and fans can watch in the stands. The Gym is so lush and green on the inside. But the plants aren't just for the Pokémon who call the Gym home; they're also used in the production of perfume. In addition to being a terrific Gym Leader, Erika is also a talented perfumer. She creates her aromas right there in her Gym.

Some of her ingredients are so potent, she keeps them in a secret safe. Beware, one of those special bottles is filled with the stinky fumes from Gloom.

CELADON CITY

This Metropolis is known for its tall skyscrapers and sweet scents. Follow your nose to Gym Leader Erika's fragrance shop. There she sells amazing perfumes like the popular Daffodil Dreams.

There is also a large department store downtown that can outfit you from wigs to shoes, or rather head to toe.

VISIT FUCHSIA GYM

KOGA: FUCHSIA GYM LEADER

LOCATION: Fuchsia City

OBSESSION: Poison-type Pokémon

In true Ninja form, Koga likes to make a surprise entrance. He takes Pokémon Training and himself very seriously, but perhaps that's how one gets to lead the Fuchsia Gym. Koga's little sister Aya studies his skill and looks up to him.

KOGA'S POKÉMON: Venomoth, Venonat, Voltorb, Golbat

FUCHSIA GYM

BADGE: Soul Badge

BATTLE FOR THE BADGE: 2-on-2

Challengers at the Fuchsia Gym need good balance and no fear of heights just to make it to the entrance. A single plank of wood connecting a deep mountain gap leads Trainers to the massive, traditional Japanese mansion that is the Fuchsia Gym. However, it's hard to tell just where you are because the Gym is unmarked.

Even if you are wise enough to realize what you're looking at, you can't just waltz in expecting to meet Koga. First, you must make your way through the mansion's network of buildings filled with many tricks and traps, such as zaps from Voltorb, invisible walls, and secret doors. Then, you wait for the real surprise to spring on you—Koga.

Once Trainers are granted a battle, they really need to keep on their toes as Koga unleashes his Poison-type Pokémon. The battlefield can take place in one of the many wooden interiors or in the yard.

FUCHSIA CITY

The Fuchsia Gym is located on the outskirts of town. But a busy train station is in the heart of the city. The track is always crowded with commuters. A very tall tree is in front of the station. A round, purple Pokémon Center with a Poké Ball painted on the roof is across the street. A big yellow "P" marks the building.

BLAINE: THE CINNABAR GYM LEADER

LOCATION: Cinnabar Island

OBSESSION: Fire-type Pokémon

Blaine has grown frustrated that his home has become more of a tourist trap than a Trainer haven. Sick of battling travelers who he claimed, "cared more about postcards and t-shirts than about Pokémon," Blaine went into hiding, closing his Gym in town and disguising his bald head.

Blaine wears a long, red wig and sunglasses so he can go unrecognized. He pretends to run a hotel called The Big Riddle. Speaking of which, there is only thing Blaine loves as much as a Pokémon battle: riddles. He loves to test Trainers' strategy and creativity. So, he never answers their questions directly. Instead, he gives them clues cleverly relayed in a riddle.

BLAINE'S POKÉMON:

Ninetales, Rhydon, Magmar

CINNABAR GYM

BADGE: Volcano Badge

BATTLE FOR THE BADGE: 3-on-3

In Cinnabar Gym's case, X does not mark the spot. The entrance fence at the old Cinnabar Gym is blocked off with a big "X" made out of wood. From the outside, it looks like a wooden wreck. It's leaning to one side, nearly collapsed. Trainers have stopped coming here to challenge Gym Leader Blaine—but that's all part of his plan! He has hidden his new Gym from tourists who would pass through just for a thrill. He is only interested in battling serious challengers looking to make their mark in Kanto.

If you want a Volcano Badge, well, you have to be willing to battle in a Volcano! The name is not false advertising. You find the way to the Cinnabar Gym by getting yourself into hot water—literally. A giant Gyarados statue resides in one pool of Cinnabar Island's famous Hot Springs. The statue is actually a lever that opens the mountain's rock face.

Then, candlelight leads challengers down stone steps to a door with a handle that is too hot to hold. This door leads to Blaine's battlefield. Suspended above a sea of lava, the rectangular battlefield resides inside the volcano. The room is very hot, and the battle for the badge is fiery. Blaine would argue that if you can't take the heat, get out of the Kanto League.

CINNABAR ISLAND

Packed with hotels and souvenir shops, it's clear that Cinnabar Island's main industry is tourism. But who could resist the allure of the city's comforts combined with the relaxing vibes of an island locale? Boatloads of travelers are dropped off here every day.

Above a park sits a little-known hotel, The Big Riddle. It has a clock tower and a very important but mysterious owner. It's not to be missed for a Trainer looking to find the local Gym.

From miles away, you can spot the massive volcano at the center of the island. The lava heats up one of the biggest tourist attractions, the area's hot springs.

The Pokémon Research Laboratory on the island is world-renowned. It's a long, thin building with a big Poké Ball sign. Inside, Fighting-type Pokémon like Machop, Machoke, Hitmonlee, and Hitmonchan train. Poliwrath have been known to work out there with the exercise equipment and pool. For years, Trainers have flocked to the lab to learn the latest Pokémon techniques. But as of late, it's become more of a tourist attraction

VISIT VIRIDIAN GYM

GIOVANNI: VIRIDIAN GYM LEADER

LOCATION: Viridian City

OBSESSION: Ground-type Pokémon

It's pretty hard to pin down Giovanni, the Viridian Gym Leader. That's because he has more business to attend to than just battles for badges. Giovanni is the owner of the island amusement park, Pokémon Land, but he's even better known for being a Team Rocket boss. Among his underlings are Jessie, James, and Meowth. But he is way sharper than his goons and he can't hide his disappointment when they fail. Giovanni cares a lot about appearance. Always dressed in a suit and tie, he likes to pet the Persian by his side.

GIOVANNI'S POKÉMON:

Persian, Golem, Kingler, Machomp, Rhydon

This terrible trio travels all over Kanto causing trouble. Look out for the likes of Jessie, James, and Meowth, although sometimes they are dressed up in disguise. Perhaps the easiest clue to spot is that Team Rocket's Meowth can communicate with humans—and the things that come out of its mouth are hilarious! But the trio is also up to funny business. They do whatever their boss, Giovanni, wants. That occasionally means they substitute for him at the Gym. But they don't play fair, so Trainers should beware.

VIRIDIAN GYM

BADGE: Earth Badge

BATTLE FOR THE BADGE: 3-on-3

A fabulous fountain sits between two elegant staircases that take Trainers up to a terrace. A path lined with columns leads to the palatial peach-colored Viridian Gym. At the doors, two warriors wearing armor hold halberds at attention. To gain entry, you must first be allowed to pass by them.

Trainers who make it inside the Gym are treated to a battle for the Earth Badge. The battlefield is lined with more columns and a stone arch. The Leader or Leaders can rise like a rock star onto the field through a special door in the floor. However, Giovanni prefers to sit in his command chair on a balcony above the battlefield.

Giovanni also has an office at the Viridian Gym. He takes meetings with Team Rocket agents from behind a big desk while petting Persian. His office has a fireplace, but most of the heat at this Gym is found on the battlefield.

VIRIDIAN CITY

Although there are many tall buildings, this city with lots of greenery lives up to its name. From anywhere in town, you can see the nearby mountains in the background. You can spot the local Pokémon Center by its big red dot, smack in the center of a half-dome roof.

POKÉMON CONTESTS

They say beauty is in the eye of the beholder. And if you like to behold beauty, look no further than a Pokémon Contest. There are two main phases of a Pokémon Contest: the performance and the battle. In the performance portion of the competition, Trainers and their Pokémon partners strut their stuff, showing off their style, skill, and finesse. Unlike other battles, Contest Battles are about displaying perfect and pretty form, not just power. In both sections of the competition, judges score Coordinators and their Pokémon partners on their heartfelt teamwork and elegant style.

The Pokémon Contest rules are as follows:

- Each contestant can use one Pokémon per round, unless the Contest calls for a double performance.

- Coordinators may switch Pokémon partners between rounds.

- Pokémon first perform in a qualifying round.

- The scores in the qualifying round determine a Coordinator's place in the semifinals.

- Pokémon are permitted to use single, double, or triple combination attacks to lower an opponent's score.

- Coordinators have only five minutes on the floor. The score at that time decides the winner.

- The winner of the Contest is awarded with a coveted Ribbon. If a Coordinator earns five Ribbons from any region, he or she may enter the Grand Festival. The winner of the Grand Festival is awarded a special victory cup and the title "Top Coordinator."

Coordinators flock to Kanto because it hosts many local Pokémon Contests. If you want to enter, just be sure you have a valid Contest Pass!

The Pokémon Contest judges in Kanto are: Mr. Raoul Contesta, the head of the Contest committee; Mr. Sukizo, the president of the Pokémon Fan Club; the local Nurse Joy; and MC Lilian Meridian.

CONTEST HALL LOCATIONS IN KANTO

SAFFRON CITY

This amazing Saffron City Contest Hall sits just outside the hustle and bustle of the city on a grassy lawn. The building itself is a dome with many arches and a round, red top. A large replica of the Saffron Ribbon—the prize awarded to the winner of the Contest—sits proudly atop the dome.

GARDENIA TOWN

The Contest Hall in Gardenia Town is an open-air arena. It is a big red dome with a circular opening and battlefield. From the arena seats, you can see all of the action and the sky. Three arches mark the entrance.

WISTERIA TOWN

The Contest Hall on Potpourri Island is located in Wisteria Town. On a lawn, in the shadow of the city's buildings, sits the golden dome of the Wisteria Contest Hall.

SILVER TOWN

Two large staircases lead up to the bright yellow Silver Town Contest Hall. The building has cool geometric angles and lots of windows, including a skylight.

CHRYSANTHEMUM ISLAND

You might want to bring your bathing suit to the Chrysanthemum Contest. The entrance to the Contest Hall is right on the beach! The huge, round arena is located at the edge of the city, nestled between buildings. There is only a half-dome roof for shade. So, with an aerial view you can see the big Poké Ball painted on the contest floor.

MULBERRY CITY

This massive arena can pack in Pokémon fans! A theater in the round, Pokémon Contest competitors take center stage below the two tiers of seating. It's hard to miss this Contest Hall. In addition to being a big blue dome smack dab in the city, it is also marked with a sign that reads "Pokémon Contest" just above a golden awning. The front also boasts a big Poké Ball sculpture marked with a "P."

TERRACOTTA TOWN

Terracotta Town is sandwiched between stony mountains and the sea. Pokémon Contests are a big deal here. The whole city is filled with outdoor vendors and excitement for the Terracotta Town Contest Festival. Since it's not an official Contest, competitors do not need a Contest Pass to enter.

The Contest Hall has a pretty pink arch front and center. The rounded roof is made entirely of windows that look out onto a forest full of fluffy green trees. The stage is rectangular with Pokémon fans watching from stands on each side. So, if you enter the Terracotta Town Contest Festival, you and your Pokémon partners better be ready to put on a show!

THE INDIGO PLATEAU

The Indigo Plateau is an important place for Pokémon Trainers, Pokémon Coordinators, and, of course, Pokémon fans who don't want to miss any of the action! It hosts two major Pokémon competitions: the Indigo Plateau Conference and the Kanto Grand Festival. To qualify for the Indigo League's top competition, Pokémon Trainers must earn eight badges in Kanto. To compete in the Grand Festival, Pokémon Coordinators must present five Contest Ribbons; the prize can be from any region. To watch and cheer from the stands, you just have to be a Pokémon fan!

THE INDIGO PLATEAU CONFERENCE

INDIGO STADIUM

With green mountains behind and a river beside it, a dirt path carved out through shrubs leads to the big Indigo Stadium. Surrounding the stadium are manicured lawns connected by a grid of roads and a few smaller stadiums where the four qualifying rounds are held. A simple fountain spouts up towards the sky, pointing toward the Poké Ball sign that marks the amazing main arena.

LET THE GAMES BEGIN!

Don't overlook a man with long, silver hair, a backward cap, and shorts as just another spectator. It could be the president of the Pokémon League Torch Committee, Charles Goodshow. He is more interested in heart than formality, and he uses his instinct to preside over the Indigo League Championship. Mr. Goodshow is responsible for ensuring the famous torch carrying the flame of Moltres ignites the stadium's central torch. He selects ambassadors to run this important torch to the stadium. When it arrives, this signifies the beginning of the League Championship.

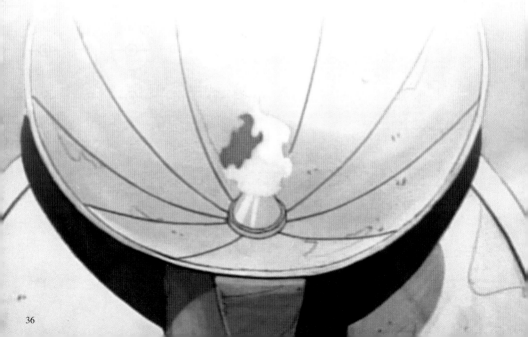

Next, the crowd and competitors are dazzled by the opening ceremonies. A flock of Pidgey is released over the crowd. Then, all the Trainers competing in the Indigo Plateau Conference parade across the stadium.

The Indigo Plateau Conference Rules are as follows:

> The first four rounds are three-on-three battles. To qualify for the next round, Trainers must win all four rounds on each of the four different battlefields: Rock, Grass, Water, and Ice. This eliminates many competitors.

> The next round features the top 16 Trainers competing in the main Indigo Stadium. To select the order of the battle, Trainers fish for Magikarp marked with their number.

> From the quarterfinals on, the battles become six-on-six. Trainers must use all of their Pokémon on hand.

At the closing ceremony, no one goes home empty handed. Every competitor is awarded a participation badge. The winner is given a precious prize: a magnificent trophy. Then, fireworks light up the sky.

POKÉMON LEAGUE VILLAGE

Pokémon Trainers stay in special housing together during the competition. This builds camaraderie and guarantees no one misses out because of a hotel reservation. It levels the playing field and allows for more fun times!

KANTO GRAND FESTIVAL

The first round is the Appeal in which all the Coordinators and their Pokémon partners get to perform a single move. Because of the large number of competitors, this round is held in two stadiums and judged by the usual three judges, plus Vivian Meridian—Lilian's sister and the Hoenn Pokémon Contest MC—as well as three more Nurse Joys. Together, they help whittle down the pool of 270 Coordinator competitors. Only 64 move onto the next round.

In this round, Pokémon Coordinators and their Pokémon partners again perform to show off their moves. And the competition is stiff!

In the following round, the remaining 16 Coordinators compete in Double Battles wherein contestants have five minutes on the clock to strut their stuff and reduce their opponent's points. It is all about the beautiful battle style of the Pokémon Coordinator and Pokémon partner. The winner receives the coveted Ribbon Cup and earns the title of Top Coordinator.

GRAND FESTIVAL CONTEST HALL

The Kanto Grand Festival Contest Hall is nestled in the valley and surrounded by trees. The main building is very tall and round with a red-rimmed dome. The stands go all the way up to the giant skylight in the center.

VISIT PROFESSOR OAK'S LAB IN PALLET TOWN

High on the hill sits this yellow lab with a giant white windmill. Visitors have to cross through the gate and go up its long staircase, but it's definitely worth the trip. This Pokémon habitat and research facility is famous throughout the Pokémon world because of its distinguished professor and all of his well-known work.

Professor Oak also cares for hundreds of Pokémon at his lab and habitat. From any Pokémon Center, Pokémon Trainers originally from Kanto can send their Pokémon pals to live with Professor Oak. New Trainers in Kanto begin their journey at Professor Oak's lab in Palette Town. There, they can pick their First Partner Pokémon.

KANTO FIRST PARTNER POKÉMON:

Bulbasaur, Squirtle, Charmander

THE CLAIMS TO PROFESSOR OAK'S FAME

Professor Oak is a researcher who focuses his studies on Pokémon behavior and how Pokémon interact with people. Through the course of his work, he invented a device that can instantly identify and describe every Pokémon: the Pokédex! Every Trainer relies on his or her Pokédex, so they are given out with First Partner Pokémon in every region.

But Professor Oak isn't only superb at science, he is also a gifted writer. Professor Oak loves to compose short prose or poems. In addition to his academic pursuits, Professor Oak is exceptional at Pokémon battles. He fights for what's right with his powerful Pokémon pal, Dragonite.

ALL IN THE FAMILY

Professor Samuel Oak isn't the only professor in his family. His cousin, Professor Samson Oak, is the principal at the esteemed Pokémon School on Melemele Island in the Alola region. The professor in Pallet Town also has a grandson who is a decorated Pokémon Trainer, Gary Oak.

PLACES FOR POKÉMON WATCHING

THE HIDDEN VILLAGE

A simple log cabin on a lake is the serene setting for a secret place for Pokémon. Here, Melanie cares for Pokémon that have been injured or have been abandoned by their Trainers. They get the rest and rehabilitation they need thanks to Melanie who collects plants to use for medicine to help restore a Pokémon's strength. She nurtures all the Pokémon that come to her habitat and welcomes them into her home to stay as long as they need.

POKÉMON TOWER

Haunted by Ghost-type Pokémon, the Pokémon Tower in Lavender Town is the perfect place to try to catch a spooky Pokémon—that is if you're not easily frightened. Brave Trainers recognize this place by its two giant horns. The Pokémon Tower might look abandoned, but that's just how the Ghost-type Pokémon like it—dark and scary.

THE SAFARI ZONE

The Safari Zone is packed with amazing wild Pokémon. Some of the Pokémon that call the Safari Zone home, like Kangaskhan, were almost extinct before they were brought here to the protected area. The zone is patrolled by Officer Jenny—make that Safari Ranger Jenny, who keeps a lookout for low-down, dirty poachers looking to steal the local Pokémon.

THE MYSTERIOUS GARDEN

Most Pokémon evolve by working hard and leveling up in battle, but some Bulbasaur bypass that norm. In Kanto, there is a top secret spot where Bulbasaur from all over flock for a very unique and beautiful rite of passage. It's a hidden place where

no people or other Pokémon go, at least not this time of year.

In the center of the ceremony is a barren tree where the Venusaur that leads this Evolution ritual lives. As soon as the trail of Bulbasaur arrive, the area's plants bloom instantly, including the tree. Then suddenly, when the moment is right, all the Bulbasaur evolve into Ivysaur. It is a sight and sound to behold! That is, if anyone besides Bulbasaur could get an invitation.

MT. HIDEAWAY

Close to Pallet Town is the mountain where Bruno, a member of the Indigo Elite Four, trains. But he's not the only inhabitant. Giant Onix are known to roam the area. You can tell where they have been because their massive bodies carve out deep paths. The Onix are so big they leave crevices almost as tall as a person in the ground. According to locals, the fertile soil in this part of Kanto causes Onix to grow even bigger than their usual huge height.

VIRIDIAN FOREST

The lush woods outside of Viridian City are covered in bushy trees and shrubs. Because of its shady and delicious plant life, it is crawling with Bug-type Pokémon like Caterpie and Weedle.

CAMOMILE ISLAND

Camomile Island is covered in grassy plains. It's the kind of landscape that so many Pokémon love. Thus, it's no wonder so many different wild Pokémon, like Tropius, Rhyhorn, Nidoran, Rapidash, and Girafarig, call this island home.

AWESOME TOURIST ATTRACTIONS

SCISSOR STREET

The top Pokémon breeders, or people devoted to learning all about raising Pokémon, have shops on Scissor Street. So, it's no wonder it's also known as Breeder's Lane. This busy block is where Pokémon breeders in the know go to find the hot, new breeder gear. The street is lined with state-of-the-art Pokémon salons, makeup stores, and fashion shops. Bring your Pokémon to get pampered!

BILL'S LIGHTHOUSE

At the edge of a cliff over the ocean is a tall, white lighthouse with a house next-door. It shines an extremely bright, color-changing light to attract Pokémon, but people often visit too because Bill, the operator of the lighthouse, is a famous and knowledgeable Pokémon researcher.

The lighthouse's massive front doors have blocks of carvings featuring powerful Pokémon, like Scyther and Ditto. Don't be alarmed if a Pokémon such as Kabuto answers the doorbell—it's really Bill in disguise. He likes to dress up in Pokémon costumes to get a better understanding of them.

PORTA VISTA

People who want to make a splash flock to Porta Vista for its perfectly blue water and popular beach. The shore is lined with high-rise hotels and seafood restaurants. This Island is near a tourist attraction you might want to skip, Pokémon Land.

BRIDGE TO SUNNY TOWN

This shortcut to Sunny Town has travelers zigzagging around. That's because this unusual bridge wasn't built in a straight line. It snakes across the water for over ten miles! In addition to its irregular road, travelers must beware of the Bridge Bike Gang. Former members include Jessie and James. Although they might seem tough at times and even quick to battle, they are willing to help travelers who need an escort across the bridge. Ask to speak with Chopper or Tyra.

DON'T BE FOOLED BY THESE TOURIST TRAPS ...

DITTO'S MANSION

Accept no imitations for this Kanto location, but you might find yourself surrounded by imitators. That's because the mansion is home to Duplica, from the House of Imite, and her Pokémon pal Ditto. Ditto, the Transform Pokémon, is a master shape-shifter. It can rearrange the cells of its body to assume any form, from Abra to Zebstrika.

POKÉMON LAND

This island boasts beautiful beaches and a picturesque forest, but that's where the real nature ends. The inhabitants of the island are luckily all fake. So, don't be afraid of all the gigantic Pokémon that roam the place: Rhydon, Zapdos, Venusaur, Kabutops, Blastoise, Pikachu, and Charizard. They are ten times their normal sizes because they're all mechanical. If you want to take a tour, a guide will show you around on a Gyarados-shaped boat. But, perhaps you'd rather save your money than line the pockets of its owner, Team Rocket boss Giovanni.

MAIDEN'S PEAK

Atop the highest cliff looking out over the ocean is the Shrine of the Maiden, a stone statue of a young woman who lived 2,000 years ago. Legend has it, she waited for her love to return from war, but he never came. She refused to move from the spot and eventually turned to stone.

Every year at the annual Summer Festival near Porta Vista her loyalty is remembered with a ceremony. A priest displays a treasured painting of the young woman. Beware, travelers can become convinced that they have seen visions in which the maiden came to them and confessed her affection. But that is just Gastly playing tricks on unsuspecting tourists!

The festival also includes a Ferris wheel, a parade of floats and costumed performers, amazing dancers, and delicious snacks. At the end of every summer, festivalgoers light candles and send them out on tiny boats to help light the way for any wandering spirits who can't find their way back home.

GET SCHOOLED

POKÉMON TECHNICAL INSTITUTE

An expensive boarding school, Pokémon Technical Institute takes the travel out of joining the Pokémon League. Instead of going from Gym to Gym to collect badges, pupils use simulators to get the experience of Gym battles under their belt. Upon graduation, they are immediately eligible to enter the Pokémon League Championship at the Indigo Plateau.

Although the path is direct, classes at Pokémon Tech are notoriously difficult. Called Pokémon Tech for short, this school often holds students back for long periods of time until they prove mastery. Many students are afraid to return home without a diploma.

There are three grades. Beginners have the same qualifications as someone with two badges; the intermediate class, four badges; and the advanced students, six badges.

The students have to wear a fancy uniform with a button-up shirt, a tie, and a jacket or vest. But polite dress doesn't always mean polite behavior. Pokémon Tech has a reputation for a snobby student body.

THE POKÉMON NINJA SCHOOL

Tucked away in the forest is a school as unassuming as its students. It's a special school where teacher Angela imparts her finest ninja training on her students along with their Pokémon pals.

You can spot students of this school by their blue uniforms, white headbands, and black belts and socks. However, it is hard to spot them when they're in action because they're trained to be stealthy. At the school they learn ninja arts such as camouflage, endurance, and the "True Heart of the Ninja."

PLACES OF DISCOVERY IN KANTO

MT. MOON

Mt. Moon stands so tall, it can be seen from Pallet Town. But the legend around the mountain has grown into an even taller tale. It is said that over a million years ago a massive meteor slammed into the mountainside. Locals call the meteor the "Moon Stone" because it landed from space. It currently is hidden in the caves of Mt. Moon and guarded by Clefairy. They protect the beautiful boulder

and collect missing fragments of the Moon Stone from the surrounding area.

The tiniest piece of this Moon Stone is very precious. Pokémon Scientists, like Seymour, have found that the Moon Stone greatly increases a Pokémon's strength. Unfortunately, there are thieves who want to steal the stone and its fragments to selfishly increase their own power.

POKÉMOPOLIS

Outside of Pallet Town lie ruins of an ancient
civilization that were once buried beneath
the rock for many centuries. It's thought that
Pokémopolis was once a sacred, hidden city
where the people built temples to honor the
power of Pokémon. Now, it's an important
place for Pokémon researchers like Professor
Dunlap and Doctor Eve, some of the foremost
authorities on Pokémopolis.

With their team, Eve and Dunlap have unearthed many unusual artifacts including a statue that
resembles Psyduck, a patterned spoon, and a stone tablet. The tablet warns those who read it:

Beware the Two Great Powers of Destruction!
The Shadow of the Dark Device will grapple with the Prisoner of the Unearthly Urn!
The Sacred City will be no more as day is swallowed up by night!
Darker still for you when they return to lay waste the world!
But no human knows the secret to soothe the Powers and guide them back to the
Shadow World.

Perhaps the biggest discovery at the site is what is thought to be two ancient Poké Balls that contain massive Alakazam and Gengar with usual markings. Is it possible that these are the two Great Powers of Destruction? Luckily, in what is thought to be another ancient Poké Ball, there is also a gigantic Jigglypuff with a booming voice that contains the antidote to protect the land from Alakazam and Gengar's fighting.

SEAFOAM ISLAND

Seafoam Island is a tropical paradise with a cool beach. Tourists come to tan and try their hand at outdoor activities like windsurfing. But serious Pokémon Trainers also visit one of the Island's inhabitants, Professor Westwood V. He is one of the Poké-ologists who programmed the Pokédex. From his lab on Seafoam Island, he studies and learns all he can about Pokémon.

DESTINATIONS IN KANTO

HOLLYWOOD

This once glamorous tinsel town has been turned into a ghost town. Although downtown Hollywood was famous for hosting fancy movie premieres with famous stars, now it has emptied out of even regular people. It seems like its best days might be behind it, but at least one man isn't giving up on the legendary city. Some movies are still made in the area thanks to the likes of acclaimed director Mr. Schpielbunk. Perhaps one man can turn this town around?

GRINGY CITY

Once a bustling factory town, Gringy City has since been abandoned because the pollution buildup ruined the air and water. Almost no one remains in the city, and those who do are treated to winds off the water that smell like sludge. But you know what really stinks? Industry dumped on this town and then left it in the dumps.

NEON TOWN

An oasis in the desert, it would be impossible to miss this bright spot. Neon Town lives up to its name with illuminated signs and spotlights covering every inch of the city. It's so bright, you can't tell if its day or night, and it doesn't even matter. Neon Town never closes—it is open 24 hours a day. People stay out all night in the casinos, attractions, shops, and restaurants. It might sound like fun, but it's made the locals pretty unfriendly. Everyone is cranky because they don't get enough sleep.

STONE TOWN

Trainers looking to help their Pokémon evolve might want to make a stop in Stone Town. It is renowned for having special stones that can level up Pokémon partners in a flash. Some Pokémon even evolve into different forms depending on which Evolution Stone is used. Take Eevee, the Evolution Pokémon, for example. Using a Fire Stone evolves Eevee  into Flareon, the Flame Pokémon. Meanwhile, a Water Stone evolves it into Vaporeon, the Bubble Jet Pokémon. And a Thunder Stone evolves it into Jolteon, the Lighting Pokémon.

However, Trainers visiting Evolution Mountain and the valley of Stone Town should keep in mind the question isn't always how to evolve a Pokémon but when. It is an important matter that should not be taken lightly. Evolution takes ability, pride, and, of course, true friendship.

COMMERCE CITY

Nothing beats the hustle and bustle of the great capitol, Commerce City! The skyscrapers and streets are filled with people and Pokémon. There is awesome shopping at the local mall, conveniently located next to the Pokémon Center. The area is filled with energy buzzing from all the activity. People, cars, and bikes are always flying by, but even they can't beat the city's notoriously strong winds.

KANTO'S COOLEST GAMES

THE BIG P POKÉMON RANCH AND RACE

Bordering the Safari Zone, this Pokémon Preserve is a place where it is against the law to capture Pokémon. So, on the protected land of the Big P Pokémon Ranch, Pokémon can grow up in the wild, totally free. This incredible area is owned by

the Laramie family who takes a lot of pride in raising Pokémon. Pokémon breeders especially love Pokémon from the Laramie Ranch because they tend to be a bit stronger than other Pokémon, thanks to their excellent upbringing. To keep all the Pokémon safe, the ranch is patrolled by Lara Laramie and her Pokémon pal, Growlithe.

The Laramie Family also hosts the awesome Big P Pokémon Race. The race starts in a stadium filled with cheering spectators, but the course takes competitors off-road and into the rugged terrain of the obstacle course. Their skills are tested to the max as they face challenges like a 45-degree uphill climb. Whoever crosses the finish line first is declared the winner and an honorary member of the Laramie clan.

THE POKÉMON ORIENTEERING
CONTEST ON POTPOURRI ISLAND

This tropical destination has many terrific sites, from Rainbow Falls to a 300-year-old tree. But if it's a challenge you seek, look no further. In addition to the Pokémon Contest in Wisteria Town, Potpourri Island also hosts the Pokémon Orienteering competition.

To test how well Trainers and their Pokémon pals work together, the Pokémon Orienteering contest has them pair up into teams to compete. Each team is given a map with five points. At each point, they must collect a stamp. To find the locations, teams are only allowed to use a compass and their map. The first team to return with five stamps wins! The grand prize satisfies both your gut and glory. The winning team receives a shiny gold metal and a super yummy supply of local fruit.

LEGENDARY & MYTHICAL POKÉMON OF KANTO

The most majestic Pokémon in Kanto are rarely seen by people or other Pokémon.
Perhaps you'll be lucky enough to spot one of these incredibly powerful Legendary and
Mythical Pokémon.

ARTICUNO:
FREEZE POKÉMON

HEIGHT: 5'07"
WEIGHT: 122.1 lbs
TYPE: Ice-Flying

MOLTRES:
FLAME POKÉMON

HEIGHT: 6'07"
WEIGHT: 132.3 lbs
TYPE: Fire-Flying

ZAPDOS:
ELECTRIC POKÉMON

HEIGHT: 5'03"
WEIGHT: 116.0 lbs
TYPE: Electric-Flying

MEWTWO:
GENETIC POKÉMON

HEIGHT: 6'07"
WEIGHT: 269.0 lbs
TYPE: Psychic

MEW:
NEW SPECIES POKÉMON

HEIGHT: 1'04"
WEIGHT: 8.8 lbs
TYPE: Psychic

BATTLE FRONTIER

The Battle Frontier is a series of intense battles for the best Trainers! Each battle is in a different location with a different, very powerful and impressive Frontier Brain. If a challenger is victorious, he or she is awarded a Frontier Symbol specific to each location. There are seven facility locations in Kanto, but only six given competitors once a Trainer registers. The seventh is revealed only to Pokémon Trainers who win all six battles and earn all six Frontier Symbols. Trainers keep their symbols in a portfolio called the Frontier Folio.

SCOTT

An agent named Scott scours Kanto looking to recruit Trainers for the Battle Frontier. He's hard to miss in his bright blue floral shirt driving a bright red convertible! Scott helps guide and might even drive talented Trainers through their Battle Frontier journey. He is full of helpful knowledge about each Frontier Brain. Scott isn't just the owner of the Battle Frontier, he's also a fan. He loves to watch the battles unfold from the stands. His main goal in starting the Battle Frontier was to expand the art of battling.

THE BATTLE FACTORY

LOCATION: Cerulean City

FRONTIER BRAIN: Factory Head Noland

FRONTIER SYMBOL: The Knowledge Symbol

The Battle Factory is a shiny silver structure with many pipes and smokestacks. The main stadium is very industrial and lined with lights that shine on the battlefield. The domed metal roof can open up to the sky.

FACTORY HEAD NOLAND

Noland is not only a Frontier Brain, he's also an excellent pilot that makes his own vehicles. Although his machines might not always work, his ability to fly gave him the opportunity to help Articuno when it was injured. Because of their friendship, Trainers could get the chance to battle Legendary Pokémon, Articuno, at the Battle Factory.

NOLAND'S POKÉMON: Venusaur, Breloom, Rhyhorn, Manectric, Golduck, Pinsir, Sandslash, Rhydon, Machamp, Camerupt, Lairon

SERGIO

Sergio is Noland's first apprentice. He helps care for Noland's Pokémon partners. During battles, he acts as a judge.

THE BATTLE ARENA

LOCATION: In the mountains

FRONTIER BRAIN: Arena Tycoon Greta

FRONTIER SYMBOL: The Guts Symbol

The Battle Arena is a big training facility with a wall surrounding it. A giant Poké Ball marks the entry arch. In the yard, Battle Arena students exercise and practice drills. Inside the main building is the battlefield lined with red columns. It has three walls and is open on one side to the yard.

To earn the Guts Symbol, Trainers face Frontier Brain Greta in a battle. But whether it's a one-on-one, a two-on-two, or a three-on-three battle, all depends on the challenger. Each Trainer gutsy enough to ask Greta for a battle gets a single spin on the wheel to decide what type of battle it will be.

ARENA TYCOON GRETA

Arena Tycoon Greta has a reputation for being a tough teacher and an even tougher competitor. From the Battle Arena, she also runs a martial arts school. Discipline could be her middle name and she does her best to impart that virtue onto her students.

Greta herself is always up for a battle challenge. She loves the thrill of the fight, so she's obsessed with Fighting-type Pokémon. Furthermore, her heroes are Fighting-type specialists Chuck from the Cianwood Gym and Brawly from the Dewford Gym.

GRETA'S POKÉMON: Medicham, Hariyama

THE BATTLE DOME

LOCATION: South of Lavender Town

FRONTIER BRAIN: Dome Ace Tucker

FRONTIER SYMBOL: The Tactics Symbol

As challengers make their way to the Battle Dome located across from the Pokémon Center, they can expect a lot of attention. Helicopters, reporters, and TV crews known as the Battle Dome Press Corps cover this Battle Frontier spot. Trainers arriving at the Battle Dome must be prepared for a tough Double Battle and a challenging press conference. But that's not all the screen time they get.

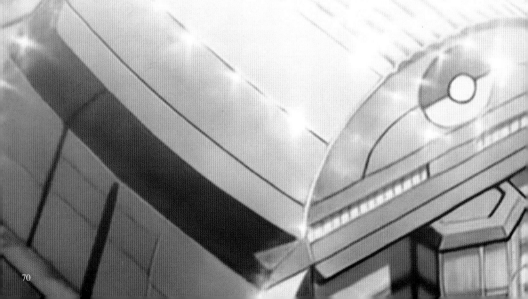

Just before the battle begins, the challenger is featured in a short video introduction. Then, as the challenger arrives on the stage, he or she makes an explosive entrance and the crowd goes wild. Tucker soon follows, flying around the arena and welcoming his crowd with confetti and fanfare.

DOME ACE TUCKER

Battle Dome Ace Tucker is a Frontier Brain and famous actor. He has lots of adoring fans he loves to entertain. Before he suits up for the stage—make that battlefield—he likes to get pampered and have his hair done like a true superstar.

A total showman, Tucker loves to perform the battle for the audience, explaining his every move. But his style isn't just for show; he is a fierce competitor to face. A decorated Trainer, Tucker won the Champion's Cup in the Orange League and entered the Indigo League here in Kanto, the Johto League, and the Hoenn League Championships.

THE BATTLE PIKE

LOCATION: Close to Fuchsia City

FRONTIER BRAIN: Pike Queen Lucy

FRONTIER SYMBOL: The Luck Symbol

The incredible place known as the Battle Pike looks very classical with all of its columns. The bright white building sharply contrasts the dramatic and modern black, red, and gold sculpture at its entrance.

Inside, the battlefield has a winding river, and its banks are filled with trees. Trainers must consider it a combination Ground- and Water-type field when challenging Pike Queen Lucy. The match for the Luck Symbol is a two-on-two battle.

PIKE QUEEN LUCY

A woman of few words, Lucy is known to be calm but calculating. She isn't shy on the battlefield—she strikes hard and fast, with confidence. Off the battlefield, she has even been known to chuck small spears shaped like a flower.

LUCY'S POKÉMON: Seviper, Milotic

BARBARA

Lucy's student Barbara is her right-hand woman. She does a lot of talking, and she believes she speaks for Pike Queen Lucy. But often, Lucy finds her words to be cruel and unnecessary, especially when she is rude to challengers. So, don't take it personally if she gives you guff.

THE BATTLE PALACE

LOCATION: Metallica Island

FRONTIER BRAIN: Palace Maven Spenser

FRONTIER SYMBOL: The Spirit Symbol

This ancient stone Battle Palace is a site to behold in Kanto. It stands in the natural wonderland that is Metallica Island. A challenger here can really celebrate the great outdoors. The Battle Palace has a massive field in the jungle that spans all the land between the river and the cliffs. So, in addition to being quick thinkers, challengers also must be quick runners to follow all the battle action at this Battle Frontier location.

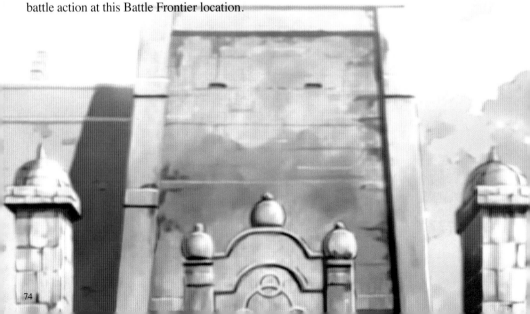

LOCATION: Metallica Island

FRONTIER BRAIN: Palace Maven Spenser

FRONTIER SYMBOL: The Spirit Symbol

This ancient stone Battle Palace is a site to behold in Kanto. It stands in the natural wonderland that is Metallica Island. A challenger here can really celebrate the great outdoors. The Battle Palace has a massive field in the jungle that spans all the land between the river and the cliffs. So, in addition to being quick thinkers, challengers also must be quick runners to follow all the battle action at this Battle Frontier location.

PALACE MAVEN SPENSER

A wise, old gentleman, Palace Maven Spenser is a Frontier Brain who really cares about Pokémon and people. This medicine man knows just the herbal or emotional cure for whatever ails them. Spenser stays in tune with nature and has a deep understanding of the way it works. Plus, he can really cook!

SPENSER'S POKÉMON:

Shiftry, Venusaur, Claydol

THE BATTLE TOWER

LOCATION: Outside Cremini Town

FRONTIER BRAIN: Salon Maiden Anabel

FRONTIER SYMBOL: The Ability Symbol

The shiny Battle Tower stands tall over the trees. The entrance is marked with an artful tablet that has a Poké Ball in the center. Inside, the multi-story stadium is lined with windows and archways with pink curtains. The match is a three-on-three battle in which only the challenger can replace his or her Pokémon at any time.

SALON MAIDEN ANABEL

This Frontier Brain has the amazing gift of being able to sense exactly how a Pokémon feels so deeply it seems as though she can speak to them. Once she gets going on the battlefield, she doesn't have to utter a word. Her Pokémon can read her mind and know her instructions. Because of this unique skill and her Pokémon pals, Salon Maiden Anabel is considered a Psychic-type specialist with psychic abilities herself. But when she does talk to them, she calls them "my friend."

ANABEL'S POKÉMON: Alakazam, Metagross, Espeon

BATTLE PYRAMID

LOCATION: Fennel Valley, near Pewter City

FRONTIER BRAIN: Pyramid King Brandon

FRONTIER SYMBOL: The Brave Symbol

The Battle Pyramid was built to Brandon's specifications and it is an impressive piece of architecture. It is a big, grey building that comes to a point. When a challenge is accepted, the point opens up so there is no ceiling on the battlefield. The sky is the limit!

The battle itself is an intense four-on-four match. If a challenger is victorious, the prizes are absolutely amazing. In addition to earning the Brave Symbol, the winner becomes Master of the Battle Frontier and a Frontier Brain candidate.

Plus, the winner is inducted into the hall of fame. But first, you have to beat one of the toughest Pokémon Trainers ever, Pyramid King Brandon!

PYRAMID KING BRANDON

Brandon is not known for his sense of humor. He's a serious guy who doesn't like intruders. He sees himself as the protector of the Brave Symbol and the underground ruins by his Battle Pyramid. He holds people and Pokémon to high standards, but he isn't a snob. He will teach the lessons he knows and help anyone in need.

BRANDON'S POKÉMON: Dusclops, Solrock, Ninjask, Regice, Regigigas, Registeel, Regirock

Kanto Region Field Guide

Written by Simcha Whitehill

The Prima Games logo and Primagames.com are registered trademarks of Penguin Random House LLC, registered in the United States. Prima Games is an imprint of DK, a division of Penguin Random House LLC, New York.

DK/Prima Games, a division of Penguin Random House LLC
6081 East 82nd Street, Suite #400
Indianapolis, IN 46250

ISBN: 978-0-7440-1963-6

Printing Code: The rightmost double-digit number is the year of the book's printing; the rightmost single-digit number is the number of the book's printing. For example, 18-1 shows that the first printing of the book occurred in 2018.

20 19 18   4 3 2 1

001-313255-February/2019

Printed in China.

CREDITS
Publishing Manager
Tim Cox

Book Designer
Carol Stamile

Production
Beth Guzman

Copy Editor
Tim Fitzpatrick

PRIMA GAMES STAFF
VP
Mike Degler

Licensing
Paul Giacomotto

Marketing Manager
Jeff Barton